A STEP INTO HISTORY™

THE CIVIL RIGHTS MOVEMENT

BY OLUGBEMISOLA RHUDAY-PERKOVICH

Series Editor

Elliott Rebhun, Editor & Publisher,

The New York Times Upfront

at Scholastic

SCHOLASTIC

Content Consultant: James Marten, PhD, Professor and Chair, History
Department, Marquette University, Milwaukee, Wisconsin

Cover: Demonstrators during the March on Washington in 1963

Library of Congress Cataloging-in-Publication Data
Names: Rhuday-Perkovich, Olugbemisola, author.
Title: The civil rights movement / by Olugbemisola Rhuday-Perkovich.
Description: New York, NY : Children's Press, an imprint of Scholastic Inc., 2018.
    | Series: A step into history | Includes bibliographical references and index.
Identifiers: LCCN 2017033471 | ISBN 9780531226889 (library binding : alk.
    paper) | ISBN 9780531230107 (pbk. : alk. paper)
Subjects: LCSH: African Americans—Civil rights—History—Juvenile literature.
    | Civil rights movements—United States—History—20th century—Juvenile
    literature. | United States—Race relations—Juvenile literature.
Classification: LCC E185.61 .R49 2018 | DDC 323.1196/073—dc23
LC record available at https://lccn.loc.gov/2017033471

Scholastic Inc., 557 Broadway, New York, NY 10012.

1 2 3 4 5 6 7 8 9 10 R 27 26 25 24 23 22 21 20 19 18

CONTENTS

PROLOGUE

C IVIL RIGHTS ARE THE FOUNDATION OF a free society. They include the right to vote and the right to fair and equal treatment under the law. The U.S. Constitution guarantees basic civil rights to American citizens. But throughout the country's history, various groups of Americans have been denied these rights.

The civil rights movement that took place during the 1950s and 1960s was the largest social movement of the 20th century in the United States. Black women, men, and children, alongside other people, battled the prejudice of an unfair society using an incredible variety of methods, from court cases, negotiations, and petitions to marches, speeches, pickets, and other protests. They fought for universal civil rights.

When we look back on America's history of civil rights progress, we often think of individuals such as **Dr. Martin Luther King Jr.** or dramatic events such as the March on Washington in 1963. Some might remember freedom fighters such as Sojourner Truth, Ida B. Wells, Frederick Douglass, or **Ella Baker**. But though these legendary people

Find out more about people whose names appear in orange and bold on pages 134–135.

of all races played enormous roles in the struggle for civil rights, they were not the only ones fighting for equality. Countless people from all walks of life joined in, making it a true mass movement. Even young children such as **Ruby Bridges** and Barbara Rose Johns were among those who pursued justice.

The civil rights movement was made up of many different voices. Sometimes they were in harmony, and other times they were in conflict, but they all sought to shape a country that would live up to its own promises of freedom and equality for all.

A sign advertises the March on Washington for Jobs and Freedom, one of the major events of the civil rights movement.

MAPS

LOCATIONS OF NOTABLE CIVIL RIGHTS EVENTS

Many of the major events that helped drive the civil rights movement took place in the southern United States, where discriminatory laws were most widespread, during the 1950s and 1960s.

Topeka
(*Brown v. Board of Education of Topeka*, 1954)

Greensboro
(The Greensboro Four begin holding sit-ins, 1960)

Washington, D.C.
(March on Washington for Jobs and Freedom, 1963)

Alaska and Hawaii are not drawn to scale or placed in their proper geographic positions.

Little Rock
(The Little Nine Rock first attend Central High School, 1957)

Selma
(Beginning of Selma to Montgomery march, 1965)

Birmingham
(Project C begins, 1963)

New Orleans
(Ruby Bridges first attends an all-white school, 1960)

Montgomery
(End point of Selma to Montgomery march, 1965)

SELMA TO MONTGOMERY MARCHES

In March 1965, demonstrators attempted three times to march from Selma to Montgomery, Alabama. Police stopped the marchers at Edmund Pettus Bridge during the first attempt. On the second attempt, the marchers turned around after saying a prayer at the bridge. In the third march, demonstrators successfully traveled 54 miles (87 kilometers) from Selma to Montgomery.

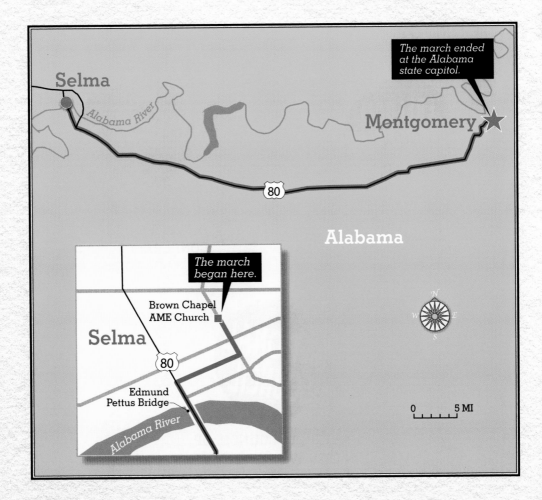

Selma

Alabama River

The march ended
at the Alabama
state capitol.

Montgomery

80

Alabama

The march
began here.

Brown Chapel
AME Church

Selma

80

Edmund
Pettus Bridge

Alabama River

N
W   E
S

0   5 MI

MAIN CIVIL RIGHTS ORGANIZATIONS

NATIONAL ASSOCIATION
FOR THE ADVANCEMENT OF
COLORED PEOPLE (NAACP)

STUDENT NONVIOLENT
COORDINATING
COMMITTEE (SNCC)

CONGRESS OF RACIAL
EQUALITY (CORE)

SOUTHERN CHRISTIAN
LEADERSHIP
CONFERENCE (SCLC)

NATIONAL COUNCIL OF
NEGRO WOMEN (NCNW)

MAIN LEGAL CASES OF THE CIVIL RIGHTS MOVEMENT

Plessy v. Ferguson
(1896)

In this case, the Supreme Court ruled that state laws requiring "separate but equal" public accommodations for black people were legal.

Brown v. Board of Education of Topeka
(1954)

In this landmark case, the Supreme Court overruled its decision in *Plessy v. Ferguson* by making segregation illegal in public schools.

Browder v. Gayle
(1956)

In this lawsuit, Claudette Colvin and several other women from Montgomery, Alabama, sued the city's mayor because they had experienced discrimination on public buses.

The first black people in America were imprisoned and brought from Africa as slaves.

CHAPTER 1

THE ROOTS OF THE CIVIL RIGHTS MOVEMENT

Though the United States promised to be the "land of the free," from its earliest days many of its citizens were subject to unjust laws and unfair treatment.

You will find the definitions of bold words in the glossary on pages 140–41.

AFRICAN AMERICANS HAVE RESISTED oppression since the moment they were first enslaved and transported to the New World in the 1600s. However, their progress was limited until the Civil War (1861–65). After the war, three **amendments** to the Constitution were approved. The 13th Amendment (1865) ended slavery. The 14th Amendment (1868) made ex-slaves citizens. The 15th Amendment (1870) gave black men the right to vote. But these new laws were often ignored or even challenged by local and state governments.

Congress also passed the Civil Rights Act of 1875. It was the first law to forbid racial **discrimination** in public facilities. But in many states, deeply rooted systems of racism remained, and black people were often prevented from voting. Violence against African Americans increased. Organizations such as the National Association for the Advancement of Colored People (NAACP), formed in 1909, worked to ensure that the country offered justice to every citizen. African Americans may have been "free" after the Civil War, but there was still much work to be done.

A family of slaves poses for a photograph at a plantation in South Carolina in 1862, not long after the start of the Civil War.

In 1956, a police officer in Jackson, Mississippi, sets up a sign to keep black people out of a waiting area at a train station. In the South, almost every public area was strictly segregated.

CHAPTER 2

JIM CROW: SEPARATE AND UNEQUAL

An 1896 Supreme Court decision declared that
segregation, the separation of public accommodations
for blacks and whites, was legal. This initiated
a wave of legislation, particularly in the South,
that made racial discrimination the law.

JIM CROW WAS THE NAME OF A STOCK character in white minstrel shows of the 1800s. Minstrel shows featured white performers wearing blackface makeup, ridiculing African Americans for white audiences. Later, the term *Jim Crow* was used to refer to the laws, rules, and customs that kept black people **segregated** from white society.

Jim Crow laws began to be passed almost as soon as slavery ended after the Civil War. In 1896, the U.S. Supreme Court ruled in *Plessy v. Ferguson* that state laws requiring "separate but equal" public accommodations for black people were legal. By 1914, every southern state had passed Jim Crow laws. Jim Crow laws made it illegal for blacks and whites to attend the same schools, swim in the same pools, or study in the same libraries. Facilities for African Americans were almost always inferior to those used by white people. The injustice of this segregation was one of the reasons that many black people migrated to the North. In many northern states, they had a better chance to escape legal oppression and find economic opportunity.

Students in the early 1900s listen to a history lesson at the Tuskegee Institute, an all-black school in Georgia that was established after the Civil War to provide quality educational opportunities to black students.

66 *There shall be equality of treatment and opportunity for all persons in the armed services without regard to race, color, religion, or national origin.* 99

—EXECUTIVE ORDER 9981, 1948

CHAPTER 3

DESEGREGATING THE ARMED FORCES

After being on the front lines against tyranny and bigotry abroad, black soldiers returned home after World War II to find that racial injustice was alive and well in America.

BLACK SOLDIERS HAVE FOUGHT FOR THE United States since the Revolutionary War, but for many years they served under different rules than their white counterparts. They were placed in segregated units and usually given support roles, such as being cooks. They knew the color of their skin had nothing to do with their ability to serve. During World War II (1939–1945), many people began pushing to **integrate** the military. For example, a black newspaper called the *Pittsburgh Courier* started a movement known as the Double V Campaign. This called attention to the fight for justice and added pressure on the government to expand the military's anti-discrimination policies.

On July 26, 1948, President Harry S. Truman signed Executive Order 9981, committing the government to the integration of the military. Now all soldiers, regardless of their race, would serve in units together. In the 1950s, President Dwight D. Eisenhower went on to set policies that desegregated military schools, hospitals, and bases. The country was slowly marching toward liberty and justice for all.

The name of the campaign came from the saying "V for Victory."

African American soldiers march through England during World War II.

Jackie Robinson's uniform and
equipment are displayed at the
National Baseball Hall of Fame and
Museum in Cooperstown, New York.

CHAPTER 4

JACKIE ROBINSON INTEGRATES BASEBALL

Jackie Robinson made history in 1947 when he became the first black Major League Baseball player. He broke the color barrier for black professional athletes in many sports.

JACKIE ROBINSON WAS BORN ON JANUARY 31, 1919, in Cairo, Georgia. From a young age, he excelled in many sports, including baseball. As an adult, he remained a star baseball player. However, the all-white Major League teams had an unwritten rule that banned black players. Robinson joined the Kansas City Monarchs, a team in the all-black Negro Leagues.

However, the Brooklyn Dodgers, a Major League team, decided to ignore the rule and signed Robinson in 1945. In April 1947, he became the first African American to play Major League Baseball. During his first year on the team, Robinson endured discrimination and threats. He was segregated from his teammates when they traveled. But Robinson thrived. He was named Rookie of the Year in 1947 and the league's Most Valuable Player in 1949. In 1962, he became the first African American elected to the Baseball Hall of Fame.

Robinson was active in the civil rights movement until his death in 1972. His groundbreaking career paved the way for countless other black athletes.

Jackie Robinson was a Brooklyn Dodger for 10 years, leading the team to six National League pennants and the 1955 World Series championship.

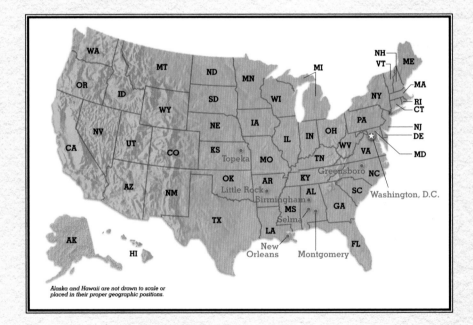

Alaska and Hawaii are not drawn to scale or
placed in their proper geographic positions.

*Most of the major events of the
civil rights movement took place
in the South during the 1960s.*

CHAPTER 5

THE CIVIL RIGHTS MOVEMENT BEGINS

Frustrated with unfair treatment, African Americans ignited a large-scale movement to secure equal access to the basic privileges and rights of U.S. citizenship.

I N THE 1940S AND EARLY 1950S, MANY BLACK citizens began actively campaigning for civil rights. The heart of the civil rights movement was in the South. That was where most African Americans lived at the time, and where racial inequality in education, economic opportunity, and the political and legal processes was most blatant. The growing civil rights movement focused on three areas of discrimination: voting rights, social segregation, and education.

On May 17, 1954, the Supreme Court overturned its 1896 ruling in *Plessy v. Ferguson* with *Brown v. Board of Education* of *Topeka*. This decision ruled that "separate but equal" was unconstitutional in public schools.

The lawsuit was sponsored by the NAACP, which often fought discrimination through court cases.

NAACP lawyer Thurgood Marshall (second from left) argued Brown v. Board of Education of Topeka *before the Supreme Court. He later became the first black justice to serve on the Supreme Court.*

Thurgood Marshall

*National Guard troops escort the
Little Rock Nine out of school to
protect them from protestors.*

CHAPTER 6

THE LITTLE ROCK NINE

Though the Supreme Court's 1954 *Brown v. Board of Education* decision outlawed segregation in public schools, some schools, such as Central High School in Little Rock, Arkansas, refused to comply.

"SEPARATE BUT EQUAL" WAS NO LONGER legal for public schools in 1954. But many schools, such as Central High School in Little Rock, Arkansas, remained all white. With support from the NAACP, nine black students tried to claim their right to attend Central High on September 4, 1957. But Arkansas's governor, Orval Faubus, wanted to keep the school from integrating. He deployed the National Guard to keep the nine students out, and crowds of white people gathered to protest against integration. The situation soon escalated into violence.

On September 24, President Dwight D. Eisenhower sent federal troops to protect the students, and the Little Rock Nine were finally allowed to start school. However, they were still subject to abuse. They were even spat on by white protesters. But they refused to be discouraged. One of the Little Rock Nine, Ernest Green, became the first African American to graduate from Central High.

The Little Rock Nine inspired more young people to take a stand. They were praised for their courage by President Barack Obama at his 2009 inauguration.

Elizabeth Eckford, one of the Little Rock Nine, walks past hostile white students in September 1957.

“*Racial integration is not going to be accepted in the South.***”**

—Senator Harry F. Byrd
of Virginia, 1955

CHAPTER 7

RESISTANCE IN THE SOUTH

Peaceful demonstrators in the South were met
with violence from law enforcement and local
vigilante groups such as the Ku Klux Klan.

A S THE CIVIL RIGHTS MOVEMENT SWELLED, white resistance also grew. Terrorist groups such as the Ku Klux Klan, a white supremacist organization founded in 1866 in the South, thrived. Local and state governments, angered by federal actions to promote civil rights, often endorsed such extremist groups.

Led by Virginia senator Harry F. Byrd, local officials attempted to block integration. They shut down schools and withheld funding from integrated educational institutions. In 1956, Byrd joined other southern politicians in signing the "Southern Manifesto," which condemned racial integration and encouraged resistance from state governments. One way states did this was by making it difficult for black people to vote.

In 1957, Congress debated a bill for a new civil rights act. The new law would establish a commission for investigating cases of possible discrimination in the voting process. Southern Democrats were opposed. With the help of Senator Lyndon B. Johnson of Texas, a weakened version of the bill was finally passed by Congress.

Senator Strom Thurmond of South Carolina spoke for more than 24 hours straight in front of the Senate in an attempt to block the vote.

Members of the Ku Klux Klan often set crosses on fire to intimidate and harass black people.

Resistance against the segregation of public buses of Montgomery, Alabama, helped draw national attention to the civil rights movement.

CHAPTER 8

CLAUDETTE COLVIN: A TEENAGER READY TO FIGHT

Tired of the double standards and injustices
of segregation, an Alabama teenager refused
to give up her seat on a public bus.

I N 1955, PUBLIC BUSES IN MONTGOMERY, Alabama, remained segregated. Black riders had to board the bus using the front door, pay their fare, then leave the bus and get back on through the back door to find seats. If seating ran out, black people had to give their seats to white riders. If there were open seats in the "white" section, black people still had to stand.

Fifteen-year-old Claudette Colvin had learned about famous freedom fighters such as Harriet Tubman. On March 2, 1955, when she was told to give her seat to a white man, she did not move. "History had me glued to the seat," she said afterward. The high school student was handcuffed, dragged off, and jailed.

Colvin wanted to fight her arrest in court, but she did not have the support of the NAACP or other organizations that provided legal assistance in civil rights cases. She pleaded not guilty, but was convicted and sentenced to probation.

The NAACP considered participating in Colvin's case but decided that because she was young and pregnant, the case would draw too much negative publicity.

Claudette Colvin, depicted here in a reenactment, joined several others in the 1956 federal lawsuit Browder v. Gayle.

For refusing to give her bus seat to a white man in December 1955, Rosa Parks was arrested and treated like a criminal.

CHAPTER 9

ROSA PARKS AND THE MONTGOMERY BUS BOYCOTT

One woman's act of resistance on a Montgomery,
Alabama, bus sparked a bus boycott that
went on for more than a year.

NINE MONTHS AFTER CLAUDETTE COLVIN refused to give up her seat, another woman stayed in her seat to stand up for justice. After a day of work at a department store, activist **Rosa Parks** was riding home in the "colored" section of a bus. The bus filled up, and its driver demanded that <u>she give her seat</u> to a white passenger. She refused and was arrested.

Parks was a well-respected community member who worked for the local NAACP. Her arrest encouraged local activists to call for a one-day bus boycott. The boycott was soon extended. A group called the Montgomery Improvement Association organized the boycott. Its leader was a young minister named Martin Luther King Jr. In reaction to the boycott, King's home was bombed. It was the first of many violent attacks against the legendary civil rights leader. He promised to "meet violence with nonviolence."

African Americans were threatened, jailed, and fired from their jobs during the boycott. Yet they persisted for 381 days. In 1956, the Supreme Court declared segregation on public buses to be unconstitutional.

Rosa Parks is often portrayed as refusing to give up her seat because she was tired from work, but she later explained, "The only tired I was, was tired of giving in."

Many African Americans participated in the boycott by carpooling or walking instead of riding buses.

A statue of Martin Luther King Jr.
stands in Washington, D.C., the
site of his most famous speech.

CHAPTER 10

DR. MARTIN LUTHER KING JR.

The most famous leader of the civil rights movement,
Dr. Martin Luther King Jr. encouraged people to
avoid violence in the struggle for equality.

In 1983, Congress passed legislation declaring a national holiday in King's honor. Each January on King's birthday, it is customary to perform acts of service that promote his commitment to social change.

D R. MARTIN LUTHER KING JR. WAS BORN ON January 15, 1929, in Atlanta, Georgia, and grew up to become a scholar and a man of deep faith. In 1953, King married Coretta Scott, who later became a major civil rights leader in her own right. The next year, he became the pastor of a Baptist church in Montgomery, Alabama. Just after his first child was born, he was called on to help organize the Montgomery bus boycott. After that, the entire nation saw him as a leader of the civil rights movement.

In 1957, King helped found the Southern Christian Leadership Conference (SCLC), a major civil rights group, and became its first president. He studied the philosophy of nonviolent **civil disobedience** and led major civil rights campaigns across the country. As his work continued, he spoke about economic discrimination as well. King called for "reconstruction of the entire society, a revolution of values."

When King was assassinated on April 4, 1968, in Memphis, Tennessee, the world lost a towering symbol of moral and social progress.

For his work as a civil rights activist, Martin Luther King was awarded the Nobel Peace Prize in 1964.

College students Joseph McNeil,
Franklin McCain, Billy Smith, and
Clarence Henderson pioneered the use
of peaceful protests called sit-ins.

CHAPTER 11

THE GREENSBORO FOUR

Inspired by the work of Dr. Martin Luther King Jr, students raised their voices in peaceful, nonviolent protest in the face of taunts, threats, and violence.

A S 1960 BEGAN, MANY STUDENTS LOOKED TO older activists to learn how to continue the fight for justice. Four freshmen at North Carolina Agriculture and Technical State University had all studied the nonviolent teachings of Mahatma Gandhi and Martin Luther King Jr. Together, they created a plan to confront segregation in private businesses.

On February 1, 1960, the four students started the first "sit-in." They sat down at a "whites only" lunch counter in Greensboro, North Carolina, and asked to be served. When they were refused, the students simply sat quietly and refused to move. Whites shouted, shoved, and poured food on the protesters, who did not retaliate. For six months, they left the restaurant each night and returned the next day. Finally, on July 25, 1960, the rules were changed at the lunch counter. From then on, African Americans were served alongside whites. Soon, countless other black college students were inspired to hold their own sit-ins to desegregate lunch counters.

College students in Charlotte, North Carolina, participate in a sit-in. The long hours of sitting gave student protesters a good opportunity to get homework done.

PECAN
UPSIDE
DOWN
CAKES

49¢

Artist Norman Rockwell's painting
of Ruby Bridges shows the girl
bravely walking past tomatoes
thrown by racist protesters.

CHAPTER 12

RUBY BRIDGES: A FIRST GRADER MAKES HISTORY

A determined first grader pursued her education in the face of hate at an all-white New Orleans school. Her courageous action opened doors for many.

ON NOVEMBER 16, 1960, SIX-YEAR-OLD RUBY Bridges had an unforgettable first day of school. She was accompanied by federal marshals and her mother to begin classes at the all-white William Frantz Elementary School near her home in New Orleans, Louisiana.

When she walked into her classroom, Ruby was the only student. All of the white parents had kept their children home because they didn't want them in school with a black child. But Ruby and her family were unstoppable. She continued to attend school, escorted by her mother and four federal marshals each day. Her father lost his job, and her grandparents lost their land because of white opposition. Ruby was the only student for the whole year, and only one teacher, Barbara Henry, stayed on to teach her. That year, Ruby never missed a day of school.

Many years later, Ruby returned to William Frantz Elementary School to volunteer. She also created the Ruby Bridges Foundation for "fostering racial healing and promoting racial equity." Her courage and continued activism made her a civil rights hero.

U.S. marshals escort Ruby Bridges out of school to keep her safe.

*In 1961, angry protesters threw
rocks, slashed tires, and set fire
to the buses used by civil rights
activists on Freedom Rides.*

CHAPTER 13

THE FREEDOM RIDERS

For six months in 1961, an interracial
coalition of activists risked their lives to break
barriers of segregation by riding buses and
trains together through the Deep South.

N 1961, IN THE ATMOSPHERE OF SIT-INS AND other peaceful protests, future congressman John Lewis and 12 civil rights activists, both black and white, launched their first "Freedom Ride." In Freedom Rides, black and white people rode together on buses across the South. This was done to call attention to the fact that many places in the South continued to segregate their public buses. The Freedom Riders were threatened, attacked, and viciously beaten by white protesters opposed to integration. More than 400 black and white activists risked their lives to ride public transportation into the Jim Crow South from May to November of that year.

Local law enforcement ignored the continuing brutal attacks, but the riders persevered. Media coverage sparked a national outcry against the violence, with many people calling on President John F. Kennedy to intervene. Finally, on November 1, the Interstate Commerce Commission ruled that segregation on interstate buses was illegal. But the violence was far from over.

A group of Freedom Riders set off on a trip from New York City to Washington, D.C., in 1961.

Martin Luther King Jr. was jailed 30 times during the civil rights movement.

CHAPTER 14

FOCUS ON BIRMINGHAM

Marking a major turning point in the movement, peaceful protests in 1963 were met with brutal police violence in Birmingham, Alabama.

I N 1963, BIRMINGHAM WAS CONSIDERED BY many to be the most segregated city in America. Since 1956, the Reverend Fred Shuttlesworth of the Alabama Christian Movement for Human Rights had been challenging racial discrimination there. But for decades, local black people had faced the staunch segregationist attitudes of Birmingham's commissioner of public safety, Eugene "Bull" Connor, who oversaw the city's police.

In April 1963, Martin Luther King Jr. and the SCLC collaborated with Shuttlesworth and local organizations on a large-scale campaign of direct action in Birmingham. Called Project C, the protests included boycotts, marches, sit-ins, and "kneel-ins" at all-white churches. Even children participated. Connor not only withheld protection from protesters but also coordinated harassment against movement leaders. After a month, more than 2,400 protesters filled the jails. King was one of them.

The "C" stood for "confrontation."

During his time in jail, King wrote his famous "Letter From a Birmingham Jail," which attracted national attention to the civil rights movement.

The Birmingham police used high-pressure fire hoses and attack dogs on peaceful protesters of all ages.

*Sculptor Elizabeth Catlett created
this bronze bust of poet Phillis
Wheatley, the first African American
woman to write published poetry.*

CHAPTER 15

ARTISTS OF THE CIVIL RIGHTS MOVEMENT

During the height of the civil rights movement, black artists used a variety of media to create work to inspire the fight for social change.

**B**LACK VISUAL ARTISTS SOUGHT WAYS TO further the civil rights movement through their work. Romare Bearden's collage *Prevalence of Ritual: Mysteries* (1964) depicted the lives of African Americans in the rural South. Reginald Gammon's painting *Freedom Now* (1965) showed images of desegregation efforts.

Jacob Lawrence, another black artist, was best known for his 1941 *Migration Series*, a collection of paintings dealing with the mass movement of black people from the South to the North in the early 20th century. His *Soldiers and Students* (1962) was informed by the school desegregation battles. Lawrence was the first black artist to have his work represented in a New York gallery.

While studying in Mexico, sculptor and graphic artist Elizabeth Catlett created art dedicated to promoting social justice causes. She was known for her posters of figures such as Angela Davis and Malcolm X. She also created artwork of Harriet Tubman and Phillis Wheatley. "I have always wanted my art to service my people—to reflect us, to relate to us, to stimulate us, to make us aware of our potential," she said.

Artist Jacob Lawrence poses with his painting Olympic Games 1972 (Black Runners) *(1972).*

Bayard Rustin (left) and Cleveland Robinson (right) were two of the main organizers of the March on Washington.

CHAPTER 16

"I HAVE A DREAM": THE MARCH ON WASHINGTON

On August 28, 1963, more than 200,000 Americans
of all races gathered at the Lincoln Memorial
in Washington, D.C., to call for government
action against racism and discrimination.

I N 1963, BLACK PEOPLE STILL SUFFERED FROM segregation, unemployment, violence, and **disenfranchisement**. The SCLC joined the Student Nonviolent Coordinating Committee (SNCC), the Congress of Racial Equality (CORE), and other groups to organize a mass demonstration in Washington, D.C., to call attention to these issues.

On August 28, 1963, more than 200,000 Americans gathered at the Lincoln Memorial in Washington, D.C. The peaceful March on Washington for Jobs and Freedom included people of all ages and races. Both ordinary people and celebrities joined in. Martin Luther King Jr. closed the march with his electrifying "I Have a Dream" speech.

After the march, King and other leaders met with President John F. Kennedy at the White House and discussed possible laws to address racial inequality. Their bold, brave steps were moving America toward comprehensive civil rights legislation.

"I have a dream that one day this nation will rise up and live out the true meaning of its creed: 'We hold these truths to be self-evident: that all men are created equal.' . . . We will not be satisfied until justice rolls down like waters and righteousness like a mighty stream."
—*Martin Luther King Jr.*

These four girls, aged 11 to 14, were the victims of a church bombing in 1963.

CHAPTER 17

THE 16TH STREET BAPTIST CHURCH BOMBING

The 1963 bombing of the 16th Street Baptist Church
in Birmingham, Alabama, killed four young girls
and showed the world the horrors of racism.

WITH THE SUCCESSES OF THE CIVIL rights movement, retaliation from white supremacist terrorists—supported by some local and state officials—continued to be swift and brutal. In Birmingham, the many explosives set off by white racists in black communities gave the city the horrific nickname of "Bombingham."

Black worshippers gathered regularly at the 16th Street Baptist Church in downtown Birmingham. A well-known center of the civil rights movement, the church routinely fielded bomb threats. Usually, the threats were empty. But September 15, 1963, was different. Just before the "Youth Sunday" service started, a bomb exploded at the church. Four little girls were killed, and many others were injured.

Mass protests followed the bombing. Martin Luther King Jr. told segregationist Alabama governor George Wallace that "the blood of our little children is on your hands." Thousands attended the funeral of three of the girls, where King spoke. Despite repeated calls for justice, an FBI investigation did not lead to arrests.

The girls' names were Addie Mae Collins, Denise McNair, Carole Robertson, and Cynthia Wesley.

Family members grieve during a funeral for the bombing victims.

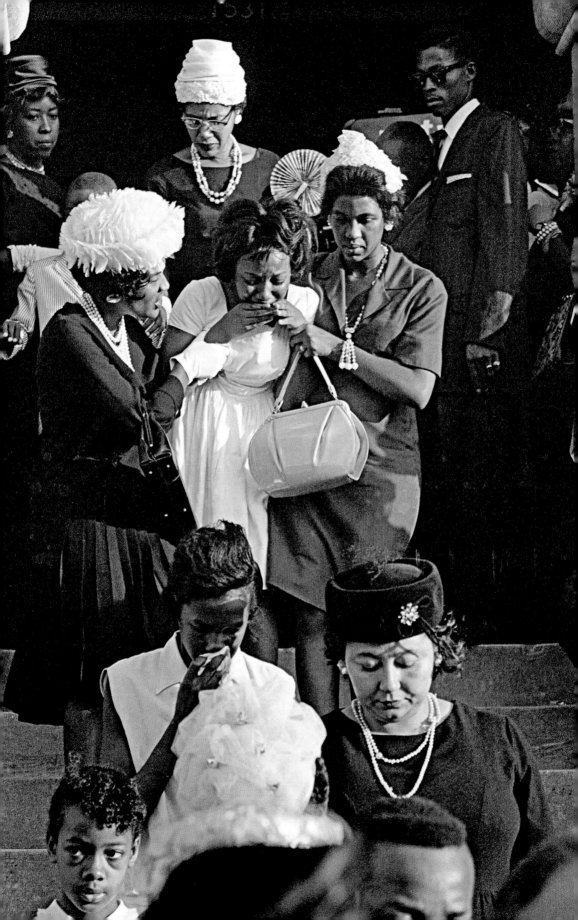

After working on a cotton plantation her whole life, Fannie Lou Hamer joined the civil rights movement in the 1950s and became an important leader in the struggle for voting rights.

CHAPTER 18

1964: THE MISSISSIPPI SUMMER PROJECT

In the summer of 1964, both black and white student activists risked their lives to confront racism in Mississippi.

I N THE EARLY 1960S, WHITE SUPREMACY HAD notoriously deep roots in Mississippi. Black people who tried to vote were often threatened with violence and losing their jobs. They were also disenfranchised by extra taxes and deceptive "literacy tests" at the polls. SNCC activist Bob Moses wanted to shine a light on these injustices.

In the summer of 1964, the SNCC and other organizations recruited white volunteers in the North to register black voters in the South. This Mississippi Summer Project (later called Freedom Summer) also created Freedom Schools that taught black history and other academic subjects.

Students also helped establish the Mississippi Freedom Democratic Party (MFDP), led by cofounder Fannie Lou Hamer. It challenged the all-white Mississippi delegation at the Democratic National Convention in Atlantic City, New Jersey, where Lyndon B. Johnson was chosen as the Democrats' nominee for president. In her address to the convention, Hamer asked, "Is this America, the land of the free and the home of the brave, where . . . our lives be threatened daily, because we want to live as decent human beings?"

Mississippi Freedom Democratic Party members demanded that their voices be heard at the 1964 Democratic National Convention.

H. R. 7152   PUBLIC LAW 88-352

Eighty-eighth Congress of the United States of America

AT THE SECOND SESSION

*Begun and held at the City of Washington on Tuesday, the seventh day of January,
one thousand nine hundred and sixty-four*

An Act

To enforce the constitutional right to vote, to confer jurisdiction upon the
district courts of the United States to provide injunctive relief against
discrimination in public accommodations, to authorize the Attorney General to
institute suits to protect constitutional rights in public facilities and public
education, to extend the Commission on Civil Rights, to prevent discrimination
in federally assisted programs, to establish a Commission on Equal Employment Opportunity, and for other purposes.

*Be it enacted by the Senate and House of Representatives of the
United States of America in Congress assembled,* That this Act may
be cited as the "Civil Rights Act of 1964".

TITLE I—VOTING RIGHTS

Sec. 101. Section 2004 of the Revised Statutes (42 U.S.C. 1971),
as amended by section 131 of the Civil Rights Act of 1957 (71 Stat.
637), and as further amended by section 601 of the Civil Rights Act
of 1960 (74 Stat. 90), is further amended as follows:

(a) Insert "1" after "(a)" in subsection (a) and add at the end of
subsection (a) the following new paragraphs:

"(2) No person acting under color of law shall—

"(A) in determining whether any individual is qualified under
State law or laws to vote in any Federal election, apply any
standard, practice, or procedure different from the standards,
practices, or procedures applied under such law or laws to other
individuals within the same county, parish, or similar political
subdivision who have been found by State officials to be qualified
to vote;

"(B) deny the right of any individual to vote in any Federal
election because of an error or omission on any record or paper
relating to any application, registration, or other act requisite
to voting, if such error or omission is not material in determining whether such individual is qualified under State law to vote
in such election; or

"(C) employ any literacy test as a qualification for voting in
any Federal election unless (i) such test is administered to
each individual and is conducted wholly in writing, and (ii) a
certified copy of the test and of the answers given by the individual is furnished to him within twenty-five days of the submis-
sion of his request made within the period of time during which
records and papers are required to be retained and preserved pur-
suant to title III of the Civil Rights Act of 1960 (42 U.S.C. 1974-
74e; 74 Stat. 88) : *Provided, however,* That the Attorney General
may enter into agreements with appropriate State or local author-
ities that preparation, conduct, and maintenance of such tests in
accordance with the provisions of applicable State or local law,
including such special provisions as are necessary in the preparation, conduct, and maintenance of such tests for persons who are
blind or otherwise physically handicapped, meet the purposes of
this subparagraph and constitute compliance therewith.

"(3) For purposes of this subsection—

"(A) the term 'vote' shall have the same meaning as in subsection (e) of this section;

"(B) the phrase 'literacy test' includes any test of the ability
to read, write, understand, or interpret any matter."

(b) Insert immediately following the period at the end of the first
sentence of subsection (c) the following new sentence: "If in any
such proceeding literacy is a relevant fact there shall be a rebuttable

*The Civil Rights Act of 1964, shown
here, was a landmark victory in the
fight for equal treatment under the law.*

CHAPTER 19

LEGISLATING CIVIL RIGHTS

On July 2, 1964, President Lyndon B. Johnson signed into law the Civil Rights Act of 1964, part of a large-scale attempt to overcome state and local obstruction to citizenship rights for African Americans.

Evers was a prominent activist in Mississippi who was shot to death by a Ku Klux Klan member in 1963.

I N A 1963 ADDRESS TO THE NATION, PRESIDENT John F. Kennedy pressed Americans for strong, definitive action to ensure justice and equality for all citizens. Numerous bombings and the murders of <u>Medgar Evers</u> and other civil rights workers had shaken the nation to its core. In the aftermath of the March on Washington and <u>Kennedy's assassination</u> in November 1963, President Lyndon B. Johnson called on the government to honor Kennedy's legacy with comprehensive civil rights legislation.

The Civil Rights Act of 1964 outlawed discrimination based on race, gender, religion, national origin, or color. It also established the Equal Employment Opportunity Commission (EEOC), which oversees civil rights in the workplace. The bill was championed by Johnson, but challenged by many in Congress. Opponents in the Senate held the longest **filibuster** in history—57 days—before the law was passed. On July 2, 1964, President Johnson signed the bill into law.

President Kennedy was shot and killed during a visit to Dallas, Texas, on November 22, 1963.

Martin Luther King Jr. and other civil rights movement leaders watched as President Johnson signed the Civil Rights Act of 1964.

On March 15, 1965, some 15,000 people marched through New York City in support of the Selma to Montgomery marchers.

CHAPTER 20

THE SELMA TO MONTGOMERY MARCHES

A March 7, 1965, march for voting rights from Selma to Montgomery in Alabama ended abruptly when state police attacked peaceful marchers.

I N JANUARY 1965, BECAUSE OF THREATS AND violence from white protesters and local law enforcement, only 2 percent of black residents in Selma, Alabama, were registered to vote. Civil rights groups and local activists decided to focus their efforts on the city.

On March 7, about 600 protesters started a march from Selma to the state capitol in Montgomery. At the Edmund Pettus Bridge in Selma, they were met by a police blockade. The police beat the peaceful marchers with batons and attacked them with tear gas. This brutality was broadcast by national media, and the day became known as Bloody Sunday.

Martin Luther King Jr. led a symbolic march to the bridge two days later. This time, the marchers knelt and prayed at the bridge, then returned to nearby Brown Chapel.

On March 21, protected by the National Guard and the FBI, more than 3,000 marchers left Selma again. They marched up to 17 miles (27 kilometers) a day and were joined by others until their numbers grew to more than 25,000. Finally, they arrived in Montgomery on March 25.

That night, three activist ministers were attacked, and one died as a result.

The march from Selma to Montgomery covered 54 miles (87 km).

Martin Luther King Jr.

Coretta Scott King

66 *I don't understand how people think they can bring anybody together without a song.* **99**

—BERNICE JOHNSON REAGON

CHAPTER 21

MUSIC OF THE CIVIL RIGHTS MOVEMENT

Many different types of music—gospel, spirituals, folk music, blues, and more—were tools for activists as they worked to sustain and build on the messages of the civil rights movement.

MUSIC SERVED A POWERFUL PURPOSE IN the civil rights movement. Traditional songs such as "We Shall Overcome," "Oh, Freedom," and "This Little Light of Mine" offered encouragement and shared messages of protest.

Martin Luther King Jr. recalled the powerful music of the 1955 Montgomery bus boycott in a memoir. Traditional church hymns and spirituals were an early movement staple. These songs expressed joy and jubilation along with intense pain and sorrow. Many activists were trained at Highlander Folk School in Tennessee, where they learned the principles of nonviolence along with songs.

The student leaders of the 1960s brought new lyrics to old melodies, singing the stories of actions such as the Freedom Rides. Imprisoned activists sang to each other across jailhouses. SNCC's Bernice Johnson Reagon cofounded the Freedom Singers, an Albany, Georgia, group, in 1962. The traveling quartet performed to raise money for SNCC and to rally civil rights supporters.

The four original members of the Freedom Singers pose with singers Guy and Candie Carawan during a visit to Rhode Island to perform at the 1963 Newport Folk Festival.

(left to right) Rutha Harris, Guy Carawan (with his son), Cordell Reagon, Bernice Reagon, Charles Neblett, Candie Carawan

Black voters in Baltimore, Maryland, line up to cast their ballots in the 1964 elections.

CHAPTER 22

THE VOTING RIGHTS ACT OF 1965

After centuries of injustice, black voting rights were strengthened in 1965 by what has been called "the single most effective piece of civil rights legislation ever passed by Congress."

I N 1870, THE 15TH AMENDMENT TO THE Constitution had made it illegal to deny male citizens the right to vote because of their race. But some states prevented African Americans from voting using strategies such as "literacy tests," which were designed to confuse people, and poll taxes, which allowed governments to charge people to vote. **Gerrymandering** was another major way local governments challenged the Constitution.

Congress continued to pass voter protection legislation, but intimidation continued. Increasing violence from vigilantes and law enforcement demanded a strong response. President Lyndon B. Johnson signed the Voting Rights Act (VRA) into law on August 6, 1965, reinforcing the 15th Amendment nationwide. The federal government now had the right to approve or deny changes states made to their voting laws. It could also keep a close official eye on local elections. The VRA had an immediate impact. By the end of 1965, about 250,000 new black voters were registered. By 1968, more than 300 African Americans had been elected to office.

After the passage of the Voting Rights Act, many African Americans in southern towns were able to vote for the first time.

A raised fist was an important symbol
of the Black Power movement, while
the colors red, yellow, and green
symbolized pride in African heritage.

CHAPTER 23

THE BLACK POWER MOVEMENT

Some activists set their goals beyond integration. Traditional strategies of protest were questioned as young people took on leadership roles and black empowerment became a focus of the movement.

A S THE 1960S BEGAN, YOUNG PEOPLE brought a new energy to the civil rights movement through organizations such as SNCC and CORE. Students were at the forefront of **grassroots** organizing. However, some began to question the usefulness of traditional marches and sit-ins.

By 1965, SNCC, led by Stokely Carmichael, called for Black Power. "Black Power" is a civil rights rallying cry popularized in the late 1960s to promote self-determination and empowerment in black communities. Another Black Power group, the Black Panther Party, was founded in 1966 by activists Bobby Seale and Huey Newton. It built black-owned bookstores, schools, and health clinics. It also sought to protect black neighborhoods from police violence. Entertainer James Brown released the song "Say It Loud! I'm Black and I'm Proud" in 1968, which quickly became a movement anthem.

At a medal ceremony during the 1968 Olympics in Mexico City, athletes Tommie Smith (center) and John Carlos (right) raised black-gloved fists in a controversial gesture widely seen as a Black Power salute.

W.E.B. Du Bois
29

Black Heritage USA

Writers and leaders such as
W. E. B. Du Bois believed that
black people could improve
their situation by studying
their African heritage.

CHAPTER 24

PAN-AFRICANISM

The desire to connect black people across the globe spread through the early 1960s, promising unity and cooperation.

I N THE EARLY 1960S, MORE THAN TWO DOZEN African nations gained independence from European nations. Leaders promoted Pan-Africanism, a philosophy encouraging black people around the world to take pride in their African identity. Two of the most prominent voices for Pan-Africanism were not located on the African continent. Writer and NAACP founder W. E. B. Du Bois wrote "the problem of the twentieth century is the problem of the color line" in his 1903 book, *The Souls of Black Folk*. Du Bois advocated for the study of African history and culture as one of the remedies. Jamaican activist Marcus Garvey founded the Universal Negro Improvement Association (UNIA) and the Black Star shipping company, which promoted a return to Africa for black people around the world. He called for "Africa for Africans, at home and abroad."

Ghanaian president Kwame Nkrumah called for a United States of Africa. The Organization of African Unity (OAU) was formed by 32 African countries in 1963. The late 1960s saw many African Americans, influenced by the Black Power movement, develop a renewed interest in the Pan-African movement.

Kwame Nkrumah (center) became the president of Ghana in 1957 when the African nation won its independence from Great Britain. Nkrumah was a vocal advocate of Pan-Africanism.

" We are nonviolent with people who are nonviolent with us. "

—MALCOLM X

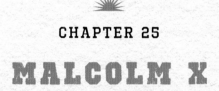

CHAPTER 25

MALCOLM X

Fiery, determined, and eloquent, Malcolm X inspired self-respect and pride in a generation of African Americans frustrated by racism and discrimination.

Malcolm X's father was likely killed by white supremacists. He had been frequently threatened by the Ku Klux Klan.

MALCOLM LITTLE WAS BORN IN 1925 IN Omaha, Nebraska. Sadly, his <u>father was murdered</u> when he was six years old. Later, Malcolm began to commit crimes. In 1946, he was convicted of burglary in Massachusetts and sent to prison. There, he turned to the teachings of the Nation of Islam, a religious and political group dedicated to improving the lives of African Americans. Malcolm joined the group, took the name <u>Malcolm X</u>, and became an advocate for black empowerment and self-defense against white violence. Malcolm's later criticism of the Nation of Islam led to a break with the group, and he ultimately embraced traditional Islam.

During a 1964 **hajj** to Mecca in Saudi Arabia, Malcolm founded the Organization of Afro-American Unity. "We are not fighting for integration, nor are we fighting for separation," he said. "We are fighting for recognition as free human beings in this society."

Malcolm X gave up the last name "Little" because it was the name given to his ancestors by slave owners.

Malcolm X was assassinated in 1965 by three Nation of Islam gunmen.

*Along with civil rights
leaders, anti-war protesters
and feminist groups were
often targeted by the FBI.*

CHAPTER 26

DISINFORMATION AND DESTRUCTION

A series of secret and often illegal projects conducted by the U.S. government disrupted the work of the civil rights movement along with other campaigns for human rights.

THROUGHOUT THE 1950S AND 1960S, THE federal government used secret programs such as the FBI's COINTELPRO (Counterintelligence Program) to disrupt civil rights organizations and discredit movement leaders. COINTELPRO targeted civil rights leaders to prevent, in the words of FBI director J. Edgar Hoover, "the beginning of a true black revolution." Using informants and spies and deliberately spreading misinformation, the government sabotaged the movement however it could.

After his "I Have a Dream" speech in 1963, Martin Luther King Jr. became a major point of focus. The FBI hid spying devices in his home and hotel rooms and attacked his character even after his murder. It also worked to widen the rift between Malcolm X and the Nation of Islam. Much of this was exposed in 1971 when an activist group stole classified documents from an FBI office and sent them to various American newspapers. The FBI was forced to shut down COINTELPRO later that year.

False information spread by the FBI led to activist Stokely Carmichael being kicked out of SNCC in 1967.

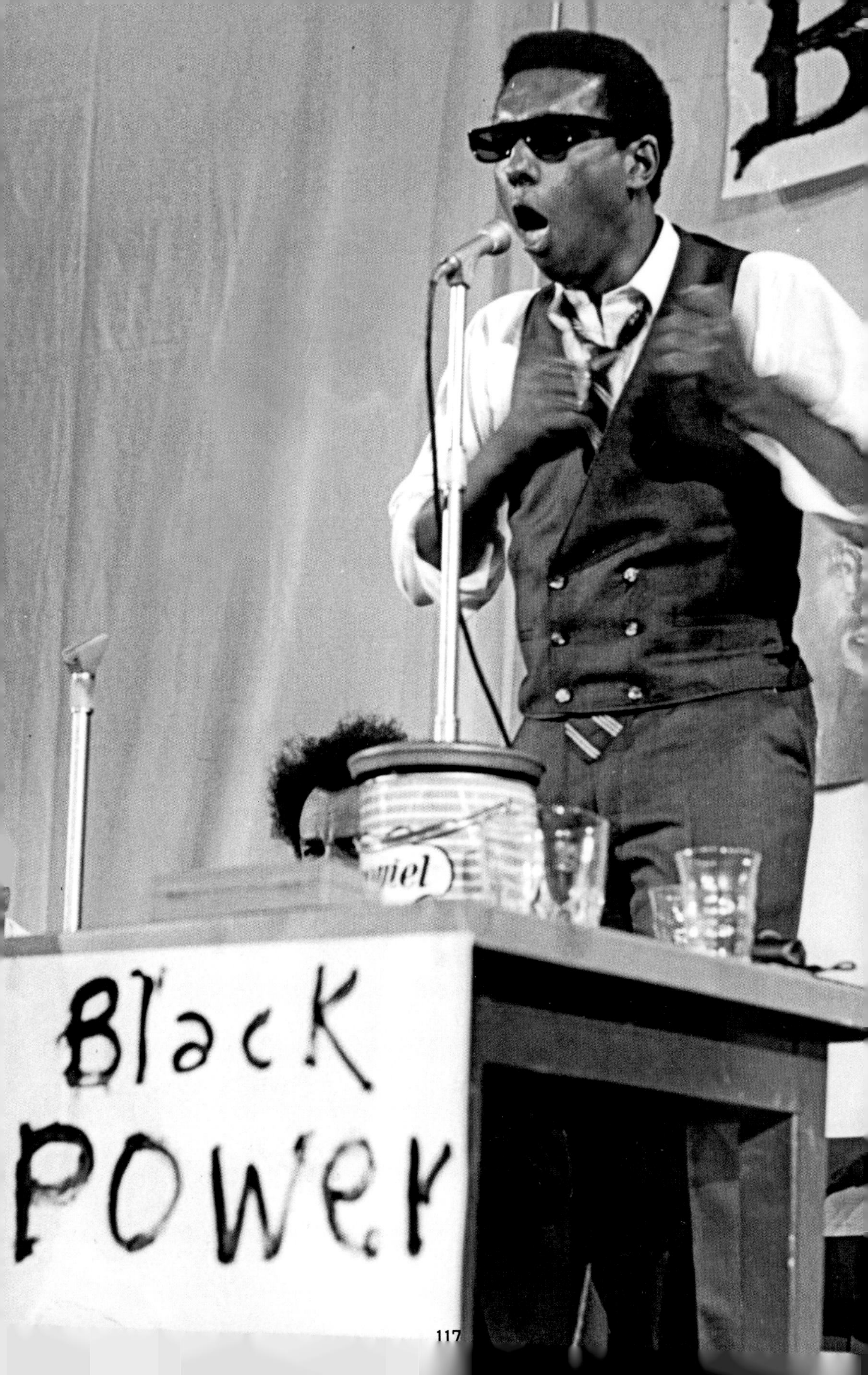
Black
POWER

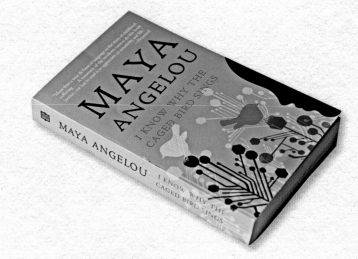

Celebrated poet Maya Angelou, best known for her 1969 memoir I Know Why the Caged Bird Sings, *worked with both Martin Luther King Jr. and Malcolm X.*

CHAPTER 27

LITERARY FIGURES OF THE CIVIL RIGHTS MOVEMENT

In the tradition of the Harlem Renaissance—the vibrant black arts movement of the 1920s—black writers in the 1950s and 1960s documented and dramatized the struggle for civil rights in America.

ARLEM RENAISSANCE POET, PLAYWRIGHT, novelist, and activist Langston Hughes came to prominence when his poem "The Negro Speaks of Rivers" was published by the NAACP in 1921. Hughes's emphasis on black pride and the celebration of all aspects of black culture influenced many of the writers and artists of the civil rights movement.

Ralph Ellison's 1952 novel, *Invisible Man*, tackles issues of identity and the social challenges that African Americans faced. It won the National Book Award for its portrayal of a black man whose color renders him invisible to white society.

In 1959, Lorraine Hansberry became the first black woman to have a play produced on Broadway, with her classic *A Raisin in the Sun*. Poet Gwendolyn Brooks became the first African American to win the Pulitzer Prize in 1949 with *Annie Allen*.

James Baldwin, one of the most prolific and well-known writers of the period, directly addressed the work of the civil rights movement in works such as *Nobody Knows My Name* and *The Fire Next Time*.

In 2012, Baldwin was inducted into the Legacy Walk, an outdoor museum in Chicago, Illinois, dedicated to celebrating LGBT (lesbian, gay, bisexual, and transgender) people and history.

"I love America more than any other country in the world, and, exactly for this reason, I insist on the right to criticize her perpetually."
—*James Baldwin*

In addition to being a singer,
musician, and songwriter, Nina
Simone played an active role
in the civil rights movement.

CHAPTER 28

YOUNG, GIFTED, AND BLACK: ENTERTAINERS IN THE CIVIL RIGHTS MOVEMENT

During the 1950s and 1960s, many black celebrities lent their fame and offered financial support to the civil rights movement.

NE OF THE FIRST BLACK ENTERTAINERS TO gain prominence as an advocate for civil rights was Paul Robeson, who spoke out against lynching and voter discrimination in the 1940s. Refusing to perform before segregated audiences, Robeson paved the way for many, including Sammy Davis Jr. Davis was one of several black entertainers who offered crucial financial support to civil rights organizations. He participated in the 1963 March on Washington along with celebrities Josephine Baker, Ossie Davis, Ruby Dee, and Harry Belafonte, among others.

Belafonte was a prominent speaker and performer during the Freedom Summer activities of 1964. He often collaborated with Miriam Makeba, a South African performer and activist. Makeba also spoke out against apartheid, the South African government's system of racial segregation.

In the 1960s, singer, songwriter, and pianist Nina Simone was notable for addressing racism in her music. She spoke at the Selma to Montgomery marches. In 1969, Simone recorded the movement anthem, "To Be Young, Gifted, and Black," inspired by the words of playwright Lorraine Hansberry.

Grammy-winning singer Harry Belafonte (right) was a close friend of Martin Luther King Jr. (left).

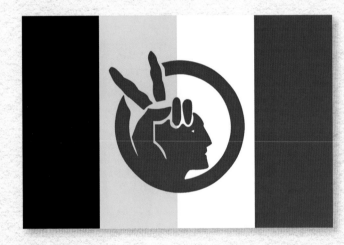

The American Indian Movement was formed in 1968 to combat unfair treatment of Native Americans.

CHAPTER 29

NOT JUST BLACK AND WHITE

Other marginalized groups—including Native,
Asian, and Latino Americans—joined the civil
rights struggle and fought to be recognized and
treated as full citizens of the United States.

S THE CIVIL RIGHTS MOVEMENT CALLED attention to injustice in America, other groups' struggles also gained prominence. Asian Americans were subject to legal discrimination by such laws as the Chinese Exclusion Act of 1882, which blocked Chinese immigration into the United States. **Internment** camps imprisoned Americans of Japanese descent during World War II. The Immigration and Nationality Act of 1965, which lifted restrictions on Asian immigration, was a major step toward progress.

In 1962, Latinos <u>Dolores Huerta</u> and Cesar Chavez organized California farmworkers into the National Farm Workers Association. The union organized large-scale strikes and boycotts that called attention to unfair labor practices.

Native Americans were not granted full U.S. citizenship until 1924. The rise of organizations such as the American Indian Movement in the late 1960s helped to address issues of discrimination against Native Americans. Government policies denied Native Americans many basic rights. The 1968 Indian Civil Rights Act restored some of these rights, including the right to free speech.

Huerta's rallying cry of "¡Sí, se puede!" became a lasting call for organizers. The phrase is Spanish for "Yes, we can!"

As a former farmworker, Cesar Chavez (center) understood the difficulties workers faced.

The election of Barack Obama, the nation's first black president, in 2008 was a major milestone, but America's struggle with racism is far from over.

CHAPTER 30

HOW FAR HAVE WE COME? CIVIL RIGHTS TODAY

Great progress has been made in the decades since events such as the March on Washington and the passage of the Civil Rights Act of 1964. However, many Americans would assert that we have not achieved "liberty and justice for all."

THE STRUGGLE FOR CIVIL RIGHTS CONTINUES today. Since the 1960s, there has been legislation in support of other issues impacting minority groups. The Americans With Disabilities Act of 1990 bars discrimination against those with disabilities, and the Lilly Ledbetter Fair Pay Act of 2009 prohibits gender-based wage discrimination. In 2015, the Supreme Court declared in *Obergefell v. Hodges* that state bans on same-sex marriage were unconstitutional.

The United States elected its first black president, Barack Obama, in 2008. However, many civil rights issues remain a concern, including **de facto** segregation in schools. In 2013, many southern states reinstituted voter identification laws that had been prohibited by the Voting Rights Act of 1965. More recently, in 2017, President Donald Trump and members of Congress moved to ban people from many Muslim countries from entering the United States.

Issues of race, class, gender, religion, and immigration continue to be pressing political matters. Many people believe that there is much work to be done before the United States can form "a more perfect union."

The Black Lives Matter movement was organized in 2012 after numerous incidents of police violence and killings of unarmed black citizens.

KEY PLAYERS

Ella Baker was a longtime civil and human rights activist and organizer. She served as the first executive director of the SCLC and was instrumental in the founding of the SNCC.

Ruby Bridges became the first black student to attend a previously all-white school in New Orleans, Louisiana, when she was six years old. On November 16, 1960, she was accompanied by federal marshals and her mother as she began classes at the William Frantz Elementary School.

Stokely Carmichael worked as an SNCC field organizer in voter registration campaigns and then as chair of the organization from 1966 to 1967. He promoted the Black Power movement in the late 1960s and was the leader of the Black Panther Party in 1968 and 1969.

Lyndon B. Johnson became the 36th president of the United States after the assassination of John F. Kennedy in November 1963. Under his leadership, Congress passed the Civil Rights Act of 1964 and the Voting Rights Act of 1965.

Dr. Martin Luther King Jr. is the best known figure of the civil rights movement. Under his leadership and with his commitment to nonviolence, the SCLC led many civil rights campaigns throughout the South. He was assassinated on April 4, 1968.

John Lewis is a civil rights leader who has served in Congress as a U.S. representative from Georgia since 1987. He is perhaps best known for his roles in leading the Selma to Montgomery marches and organizing the 1963 March on Washington for Jobs and Freedom.

Rosa Parks was an activist in Montgomery, Alabama, who famously refused to give up her seat on a bus for a white passenger in 1955. Her action persuaded local civil rights groups that the time was right for launching a bus boycott, which led to the end of segregation on Montgomery's public buses.

Malcolm X was an activist who embraced the Nation of Islam. He is best known as an advocate for self-defense against white violence. He left the Nation of Islam in 1964 and became an orthodox Muslim. He was shot and killed in 1965.

CIVIL RIGHTS TIMELINE

1909

The National Association for the Advancement of Colored People (NAACP) is founded.

DECEMBER 5

The Montgomery bus boycott begins after Rosa Parks is arrested for refusing to give up her seat on a city bus to a white man.

1909   **1947**   **1954**   **1955**   **1956**

APRIL 15

Jackie Robinson becomes the first African American to play Major League Baseball.

MAY 17

In Brown v. Board of Education of Topeka, the Supreme Court overturns Plessy v. Ferguson, deciding that "separate but equal" is unconstitutional.

JANUARY 10
The Southern Christian Leadership Conference (SCLC) is formed, with Martin Luther King Jr. as its first president.

FEBRUARY 1
Four black college students known as the Greensboro Four begin a campaign of sit-ins at North Carolina lunch counters.

NOVEMBER 16
Ruby Bridges becomes the first black student at William Frantz Elementary School in New Orleans, Louisiana.

1957 ... **1960** J F M A M J J A S O N D **1961** J F M A M J J A S O N D

SEPTEMBER 9
The Civil Rights Act of 1957, which focuses on voting rights, is passed.

SEPTEMBER 24
Nine black students known as the Little Rock Nine have to be escorted by federal troops to attend the previously all-white Central High School in Little Rock, Arkansas.

APRIL
Inspired by student-led sit-ins, the Student Nonviolent Coordinating Committee (SNCC) is formed at Shaw University in Raleigh, North Carolina.

MAY 4
The first Freedom Rides are held.

1962

Cesar Chavez and Dolores Huerta found the National Farm Workers Association (later the United Farm Workers of America) and organize to win bargaining power for immigrant farmworkers.

APRIL 3

The SCLC's campaign to dismantle segregation in Birmingham, Alabama, begins with a series of sit-ins, marches, and other demonstrations..

JUNE 28

Malcolm X announces the founding of the Organization of Afro-American Unity to fight for the rights of African Americans and promote cooperation with Africans around the world.

SEPTEMBER 15

White terrorists bomb the 16th Street Baptist Church in Birmingham, Alabama, killing four young girls.

1962   **1963** J F M A M J J A S O N D **1964** J F M A M J J A S O N D

AUGUST 28

Martin Luther King Jr. delivers his famous "I Have a Dream" speech at the March on Washington for Jobs and Freedom.

JULY 2

The Civil Rights Act of 1964 outlaws discrimination based on race, color, religion, sex, or national origin.

FEBRUARY 21

*Malcolm X is
assassinated.*

APRIL 4

*Martin Luther King
Jr. is assassinated.*

AUGUST 6

*President Lyndon B.
Johnson signs the
Voting Rights Act.*

1965 J F M A M J J A S O N D **1966** J F M A M J J A S O N D **1967** J F M A M J J A S O N D **1968** J F M A M J J A

MARCH 21

*Martin Luther King Jr.
leads thousands of
nonviolent demonstrators
on a five-day march from
Selma to Montgomery
in Alabama.*

OCTOBER 15

*The Black Panther Party
is founded by Bobby Seale
and Huey Newton to protect
black neighborhoods
from police brutality.*

GLOSSARY

- **amendments** (uh-MEND-muhnts) *noun* changes made to laws or legal documents

- **civil disobedience** (SIV-uhl dis-oh-BEE-dee-uhns) *noun* the act of disobeying a law on the grounds of moral or political principle

- **de facto** (DUH FAK-toh) *adjective* a Latin term meaning "in fact" that is used to refer to what actually happens, rather than what is supposed to be according to the law

- **discrimination** (dis-krim-uh-NAY-shuhn) *noun* unjust treatment of a particular group

- **disenfranchisement** (dis-en-FRAN-chyze-muhnt) *noun* the practice of making it difficult or impossible for an individual or group to vote

- **filibuster** (FIL-uh-bus-tur) *noun* an effort made by members in a representative assembly (such as the U.S. Congress) to prolong debate to delay a vote

- **gerrymandering** (JARE-ee-man-dur-ing) *noun* the reorganizing of election districts by the party in power for its own political advantage

- **grassroots** (GRAS-roots) *adjective* relating to ordinary or common people, as in a grassroots organization

- **hajj** (HAZH) *noun* an annual religious trip for Muslims to the holy city of Mecca, Saudi Arabia

- **integrate** (IN-tuh-grayt) *verb* to end segregation by allowing blacks and whites to use the same facilities

- **internment** (in-TURN-muhnt) *noun* widespread imprisonment of a group of people

- **segregated** (SEG-ruh-gay-tid) *adjective* set apart or separated from the majority; in the Jim Crow era, black people and other racial minorities were segregated from whites by law

FIND OUT MORE

BOOKS

Levinson, Cynthia. *We've Got a Job: The 1963 Birmingham Children's March*. Atlanta: Peachtree Publishers, 2011.

Lewis, John, and Andrew Aydin. *March*. Marietta, GA: Top Shelf Productions, 2013.

Pinkney, Andrea Davis. *Let It Shine: Stories of Black Women Freedom Fighters*. San Diego: Harcourt, 2000.

Tonatiuh, Duncan. *Separate Is Never Equal: Sylvia Mendez and Her Family's Fight for Desegregation*. New York: Abrams Books for Young Readers, 2014.

FILMS

The Black Power Mixtape 1967–1975 (2011)

Eyes on the Prize I and II (1987, 1990)

4 Little Girls (1997)

King: A Filmed Record (1970)

Selma (2014)

NOTE: *Some books and films may not be appropriate for younger viewers.*

VISIT THIS SCHOLASTIC WEBSITE FOR MORE INFORMATION ABOUT **CIVIL RIGHTS**

www.factsfornow.scholastic.com

Enter the keywords **CIVIL RIGHTS**

INDEX

ABOUT THE AUTHOR

Olugbemisola Rhuday-Perkovich is the author of *8th Grade Superzero*, which was named a Notable Book for a Global Society and a Notable Social Studies Trade Book for Young People. She is the coauthor of the middle-grade novel *Two Naomis*, which was nominated for an NAACP Image Award and is a Junior Library Guild Selection. She holds an MA in education, and writes frequently on literacy-related topics.